To sophia
from Kenisha

I would like to sincerely thank the following individuals for financially backing this project: Christiane Sombi, Fiona Bolger, Florence Dubach Lausch, Geraldine Grifoni, Nithy Kasa, Robin Hanan, Serge Bibangu Kabongo and Teija Ruottinen.

I would also like to express my special thanks and gratitude to Molly O'Duffy for her exceptional contribution in the review process.

Copyrights © Kensika Monshengwo 2017
Copyrights © Colette Mpia Akomuni 2017

Illustrated by Maa Illustrations.

Okani
and the
Crocodile
Queendom

Once upon a time in a little village, Okani and her friends were on their way to the river, laughing and singing with their baskets full of clothes.

One of them, named Monka, was wearing a beautiful golden ring with a sapphire stone. "Could I try on your ring?" asked Okani. "Of course", replied Monka, smiling.

At the river, Okani quickly washed the clothes from her basket and then jumped into the water. She enjoyed swimming and playing in the water while her friends were still slamming their clothes on the big rock near the river.

When they were about to return to the village, Monka asked Okani for her ring back.
Okani looked at her finger and realised that the ring was no longer there.
"It must have fallen into the water while I was swimming", Okani replied sadly.
Monka got very angry. "You must give me back my ring", she shouted.
"I am so sorry", replied Okani. "I will tell my mother and she will buy you another ring".
"No", insisted Monka. "I want you to give me back my ring, not another ring."

Back in the village, Okani's mother and father begged Monka for forgiveness and promised to buy her another ring to replace the lost one, but Monka categorically refused.
"We don't want a replacement ring", Monka's mother yelled, "I want my daughter's ring back".

The village chief called the elders and the warriors to discuss the matter under the palaver tree. After a heated discussion, they finally reached a decision. Okani must go back to the river alone and search for the lost ring. Okani's parents protested and wanted to accompany her, but the village chief and the warriors stopped them in their tracks. "She must go alone", the chief commanded. Okani's parents watched sadly as Okani took the path leading to the river.

Okani got into the water, swimming and searching desperately for the ring at the bottom of the river.

She came across a big fish. "Hello, what's your name?" asked Okani. "My name is Dusky Grouper", replied the fish. "Little girl, it's getting late and you should not be wandering in the river at this time. Please go back home", advised Dusky Grouper.

"I can't. I am looking for a golden ring with a sapphire stone. Have you seen it?" enquired Okani. "Yes, I saw a golden ring with a sapphire stone rolling in that direction. Just follow the stream", Dusky Grouper responded. "Thank you", said Okani.

Okani kept on swimming and came face to face with a turtle. "I recognise you", said Okani, "Your name is Leatherback the Turtle". "Yes indeed", replied Leatherback the Turtle.

"To what do I owe the honour of your presence in my quarters?" continued Leatherback the Turtle in a distinguished voice.

"Have you seen a golden ring with a sapphire stone around here?" asked Okani.

"Coincidentally, I have just seen it a minute ago rolling in that direction", replied Leatherback the Turtle. "I am afraid you must go home now. This place is not safe for a little girl", he added, frowning

Darkness fell across the river. Okani bumped into a hippopotamus. "What is your name?" she asked. "My official name is Hippopotamus, but my friends call me Hippo", answered the hippopotamus. "Have you seen a golden ring with a sapphire stone rolling around here?" enquired Okani. "Yes, one minute ago I saw a golden ring with a sapphire stone rolling in the direction of the Crocodile's Queendom", replied Hippo.

They had not finished their conversation when suddenly Okani got sucked up by an underwater whirlpool and spun around until she became completely disorientated.

She finally landed in front of a beautiful and luxurious gate. The water had disappeared and Okani could now breathe normally. She had reached the Crocodile Queendom, mentioned earlier by Hippo. The gate was guarded by two crocodiles dressed as warriors.

"What do you want?" shouted one of the crocodile guards.

"I am looking for a golden ring with a sapphire stone", Okani replied, "Have you seen it?"

"This is the crocodile Queendom. Little girls are not allowed in here", grumbled the second guard.

Queen Crocodile, ruler of the underwater world, appeared at the gate.

"What are you doing in my Queendom, little girl?" yelled the Crocodile Queen.

"I am looking for a golden ring with a sapphire stone", answered Okani with confidence. "Have you seen it?"

"Everything that enters my Queendom is mine", replied Queen Crocodile, "Your ring is now in my possession".

"Please could you give it back to me, so that I can go back home? It is very late and my parents must be very worried by now", implored Okani.

"I am willing to give you your ring back on one condition", said the Queen. "What is it?" asked Okani. "You see, I am the strongest crocodile in my Queendom, but I don't know how to read or write. Do you know how to read and write?" asked Queen Crocodile, slightly embarrassed. "Yes of course", replied Okani proudly. "In that case, you need to stay here in my underwater world and teach me how to read and write. Only then will I return your ring and let you go back to your home", explained Queen Crocodile. "I have no choice but to accept your offer as I cannot go back to the village without the golden ring", replied Okani sadly.

Okani's parents had lost hope of ever seeing her again. They thought that she had drowned in the river.
Okani spent one month teaching Queen Crocodile to read and write.

Everybody loved Okani in the crocodile Queendom;
she was treated like a princess.

By the end of the month, Queen Crocodile had made
a lot of progress in her reading and writing.

"I am afraid I must go home now. I miss my family",
declared Okani to Queen Crocodile.

"With my magical powers, I will send a dream to
your parents to let them know that you are coming
back", said the Queen.

Queen Crocodile returned the ring to Okani in front
of all the crocodiles in the Quendom.

Okani jumped with joy, she was so happy. The entire
Crocodile Queendom came to bid her farewell.

Meanwhile in the village, Okani's parents both had the same strange dream, in which Okani was telling them to go to the river in the morning.

They woke up early next day and ran to the river, just in case the dream was true. By the riverside, they saw a big treasure chest floating on the water. When it came near them, they pulled it out of the water and onto dry land.

They opened it and saw Okani inside the box surrounded by a very large number of golden rings, decorated with precious multi-coloured stones. They were overwhelmed with joy.

When they reached the village, everybody came out to see Okani. The entire village was cheering for her.

Okani called her friend Monka and returned the lost ring to her. She even gave her another ring as a present. "I have many rings now", said Okani, smiling.

Monka felt ashamed and left the scene accompanied by her mother.
Okani's mother turned to her and said:
"Sometimes a misfortune can turn out to be a blessing in disguise".

A portion of the proceeds from the sale of this book will go to creating better living conditions for Women & Children in the Democratic Republic of Congo, through the organisation Mwasi Ya Kilo LTD.

Mwasi Ya Kilo LTD
44 Huntstown Court,
Blanchardstown,Dublin 15.
D15 YDY6
Ireland

Email: info@mwasiyakilo.org
www.mwasiyakilo.org

Printed in Poland
by Amazon Fulfillment
Poland Sp. z o.o., Wrocław

59244524R00016